FIKA MOMENTS

Indulge in the Delights of Swedish Coffee and Pastries

DESTINY J. LEON

COPYRIGHT

Copyright © 2024 by DESTINY J. LEON
All rights reserved.

No part of this book may be duplicated, stored in a retrieval system, or transmitted using any technology, including electronic, mechanical, photocopying, recording, or other methods, without the publisher's prior written consent.

TABLE OF CONTENTS

CHAPTER 1: INTRODUCTION TO FIKA
    WHAT IS FIKA?
    HISTORY AND ORIGINS OF FIKA
IMPORTANCE OF FIKA IN SWEDISH CULTURE
    HOW TO HOST A FIKA GATHERING
CHAPTER 2 : SWEET TREATS
        Kanelbullar (Swedish Cinnamon Buns)
        Mandelkaka (Swedish Almond Cake)
        Kladdkaka (Ooey-Gooey Chocolate Cake)
        Semlor (Swedish Shrovetide Buns)
        Vaniljbullar (Vanilla Cardamom Buns)
        Prinsesstårta (Swedish Princess Cake)
        Mazariner (Almond Tartlets)
        Chokladbollar (Chocolate Balls)
        Spettekaka (Swedish Tree Cake)
        Toscakaka (Almond Cake with Caramel Glaze)
        Rulltårta (Swiss Roll)
        Dammsugare (Vacuum Cleaner Pastries)
        Wienerbröd (Danish Pastries)
        Lussekatter (Saffron Buns)
        Pepparkakor (Gingerbread Cookies)
        Havreflarn (Oatmeal Cookies)
        Drömmar (Coconut Macaroons)
        Snickerdoodles (Swedish Spritz Cookies)
        Kolabullar (Caramel Buns)
        Kardemummabullar (Cardamom Buns)
        Chokladbollskaka (Chocolate Ball Cake)
        Äppelpaj (Apple Pie)
        Blåbärspaj (Blueberry Pie)
        Rabarberpaj (Rhubarb Pie)
        Krusbärspaj (Gooseberry Pie)

- Lingonberry Pie
- Smulpaj (Crumble Pie)

CHAPTER 3: SAVORY BITES
- Smörgåstårta (Swedish Sandwich Cake)
- Köttbullar (Swedish Meatballs)
- Gravad Lax (Cured Salmon)
- Janssons Frestelse (Anchovy Potato Casserole)
- Husmanskost (Traditional Swedish Fare)
- Sill (Pickled Herring)
- Räkmacka (Shrimp Sandwich)
- Äggsmörgås (Egg Sandwich)
- Tunnbrödsrulle (Swedish Wrap)
- Pitepalt (Potato Dumplings)
- Kroppkakor (Boiled Potato Dumplings)
- Raggmunk (Potato Pancakes)
- Isterband (Swedish Sausage)
- Blodpudding (Blood Pudding)
- Leverpastej (Liver Pâté)
- Falukorv (Swedish Sausage)
- Surkål (Sauerkraut)
- Rödbetssallad (Beetroot Salad)
- Potatissallad (Potato Salad)

CHAPTER 4: BEVERAGES
- Fika Coffee
- Tea
- Glögg (Mulled Wine)
- Julmust (Swedish Christmas Soda)
- Lingonberry Juice
- Elderflower Cordial
- Raspberry Lemonade
- Apple Cider
- Hot Chocolate
- Eggnog

CHAPTER 5: LIFESTYLE AND CULTURE

FIKA ETIQUETTE
THE ART OF HYGGE
FIKA IN DAILY LIFE
FIKA AROUND THE WORLD
CONCLUSION

CHAPTER 1: INTRODUCTION TO FIKA

WHAT IS FIKA?

Fika (pronounced fee-ka) is a Swedish social custom that involves taking a break to enjoy a cup of coffee (or tea) and a pastry or light snack with friends or colleagues. It is a central part of Swedish culture and is seen as an important way to socialize and connect with others.

Fika can be enjoyed at any time of day, but it is most commonly done in the morning or afternoon. It is often held in a cozy and relaxed setting, such as a café, a home, or a workplace break room.

During fika, people typically chat about their day, share news, and catch up with each other. It is a time to relax, de-stress, and enjoy the moment.

Fika is more than just a coffee break. It is a social ritual that is deeply ingrained in Swedish culture. It is a way to connect with others, build relationships, and foster a sense of community.

KEY ELEMENTS OF FIKA

Coffee (or tea): Coffee is the most common drink enjoyed during fika, but tea is also popular.

Pastry or light snack: Fika is typically accompanied by a pastry or light snack, such as a cinnamon bun, a cookie, or a sandwich.

Social interaction: Fika is a social event. It is a time to chat, catch up with friends, and build relationships.

Relaxation: Fika is a time to relax and de-stress. It is a break from the hustle and bustle of everyday life.

Fika is a cherished tradition in Sweden and is enjoyed by people of all ages. It is a way of life that embodies the Swedish values of coziness, community, and balance.

HISTORY AND ORIGINS OF FIKA

The origins of fika can be traced back to the early 19th century, when coffee became widely available in Sweden. At that time, coffee was a luxury item that was enjoyed by the upper classes. However, as coffee became more affordable, it began to be enjoyed by people of all social classes.

In the late 19th and early 20th centuries, fika became increasingly popular as a way to socialize and connect with others. It was during this time that the tradition of pairing coffee with a pastry or light snack became common.

Fika was also seen as a way to boost productivity. In the early 20th century, many Swedish workplaces began offering fika breaks to their employees. This was seen as a way to give workers a chance to rest and socialize, which would ultimately lead to increased productivity.

Today, fika is an integral part of Swedish culture. It is enjoyed by people of all ages and is seen as an important way to socialize and connect with others. Fika is also seen as a way to relax and de-stress, and it is often used as a way to celebrate special occasions.

KEY MOMENTS IN THE HISTORY OF FIKA

Early 19th century: Coffee has become widely available in Sweden.
Late 19th century: Fika has become popular as a way to socialize and connect with others.
Early 20th century: The tradition of pairing coffee with a pastry or light snack has become common.
Mid-20th century: Fika has become a common practice in Swedish workplaces.
Today: Fika is an integral part of Swedish culture and is enjoyed by people of all ages.

Fika is a cherished tradition in Sweden and is a testament to the Swedish values of coziness, community, and balance.

IMPORTANCE OF FIKA IN SWEDISH CULTURE

Fika is deeply ingrained in Swedish culture and is seen as an important way to socialize, connect with others, and foster a sense of community. It is a way of life that embodies the Swedish values of coziness, community, and balance.

Here are some of the key reasons why fika is so important in Swedish culture:

Socialization: Fika is a social event. It is a time to chat, catch up with friends, and build relationships. It is seen as a way to strengthen social bonds and maintain a sense of community.

Relaxation: Fika is a time to relax and de-stress. It is a break from the hustle and bustle of everyday life. It is a chance to sit down, enjoy a cup of coffee, and chat with friends.

Community: Fika is a way to foster a sense of community. It is a time to come together with others and share stories, laughter, and good company.

Balance: Fika is seen as a way to achieve balance in life. It is a way to take a break from work or other obligations and focus on the simple things in life. It is a way to recharge and come back to your tasks feeling refreshed and rejuvenated.

Fika is more than just a coffee break. It is a social ritual that is deeply ingrained in Swedish culture. It is a way to connect with others, build relationships, and foster a sense of community.

Examples of the importance of fika in Swedish culture

- Many Swedish workplaces have a designated fika break in the morning and afternoon.
- Fika is often used as a way to celebrate special occasions, such as birthdays and holidays.
- Fika is a common way to socialize with friends and family.
- Fika is seen as a way to relax and de-stress.

Fika is a cherished tradition in Sweden and is a testament to the Swedish values of coziness, community, and balance.

HOW TO HOST A FIKA GATHERING

Hosting a fika gathering is a great way to connect with friends, family, and colleagues. Here are a few tips on how to host a successful fika:

1. Choose a cozy and relaxed setting. Fika is all about relaxation and socializing, so choose a setting that is comfortable and inviting. Your home, a café, or a park are all good options.

2. Invite your guests. Fika is typically enjoyed with a small group of people, so invite your closest friends, family members, or colleagues.

3. Prepare some fika treats. The most important part of fika is the food! Prepare a variety of pastries, cookies, or sandwiches to share with your guests. You can also serve fruit, yogurt, or granola.

4. Brew some coffee or tea. Coffee is the traditional drink of choice for fika, but tea is also popular. Brew a pot of your favorite coffee or tea and serve it in cozy mugs.

5. Set the mood. Create a cozy and inviting atmosphere by lighting candles, playing some soft music, and putting out some flowers.

6. Relax and enjoy! Fika is all about taking a break from the hustle and bustle of everyday life and enjoying the moment. Relax, chat with your guests, and savor the delicious food and drinks.

Here are some additional tips for hosting a fika gathering:
- If you are hosting fika at home, make sure to have plenty of comfortable seating.
- Provide a variety of food and drinks to accommodate different tastes.
- Don't be afraid to experiment with different fika treats.
- Encourage your guests to socialize and chat.
- Relax and enjoy the moment! Fika is all about taking a break and enjoying the company of others.

Fika is a cherished tradition in Sweden and is a great way to connect with others and foster a sense of community.

CHAPTER 2 : SWEET TREATS

Kanelbullar (Swedish Cinnamon Buns)

Description: Kanelbullar is a classic Swedish pastry that is perfect for fika. They are made with a sweet dough that is rolled up with cinnamon and sugar, then baked until golden brown.

Ingredients

- 1 cup (2 sticks) unsalted butter, softened
- 1/2 cup granulated sugar
- 1 teaspoon ground cardamom
- 1/4 teaspoon salt
- 1/2 cup warm milk (110-115°F)
- 1 packet (2 1/4 teaspoons) active dry yeast
- 2 large eggs
- 3 cups all-purpose flour, plus more for dusting

Filling

- 1/2 cup granulated sugar
- 1 tablespoon ground cinnamon

Instructions

1. In the bowl of a stand mixer fitted with the paddle attachment, cream together the butter, granulated sugar, cardamom, and salt until light and fluffy.
2. In a small bowl, whisk together the warm milk and yeast. Let stand for 5 minutes, or until the yeast is foamy.
3. Add the eggs to the butter mixture one at a time, then add the yeast mixture. Mix until well combined.
4. Gradually add the flour, 1 cup at a time, until the dough comes together and forms a ball.
5. Turn the dough out onto a lightly floured surface and knead for 5-7 minutes, or until the dough is smooth and elastic.
6. Place the dough in a lightly greased bowl, cover with plastic wrap, and let rise in a warm place for 1 hour, or until the dough has doubled in size.

7. While the dough is rising, make the filling by combining the granulated sugar and cinnamon in a small bowl.
8. Once the dough has risen, punch it down and turn it out onto a lightly floured surface. Roll out the dough into a rectangle that is about 12x18 inches.
9. Spread the filling evenly over the dough, leaving a 1-inch border around the edges.
10. Starting from the long side, roll up the dough tightly. Pinch the edges to seal.
11. Cut the roll into 12 equal pieces and place them on a baking sheet lined with parchment paper.
12. Cover the rolls with plastic wrap and let rise in a warm place for 30 minutes, or until the rolls have doubled in size.
13. Preheat the oven to 375°F (190°C).
14. Bake the rolls for 15-20 minutes, or until they are golden brown.
15. Let the rolls cool slightly before serving.

NUTRITIONAL FACTS
- Calories: 300
- Fat: 15 grams
- Carbohydrates: 40 grams
- Protein: 5 grams

Mandelkaka (Swedish Almond Cake)

Description: Mandelkaka is a moist and flavorful almond cake that is perfect for fika. It is made with ground almonds, sugar, and eggs, and is often flavored with vanilla or almond extract.

Ingredients

- 1 cup (2 sticks) unsalted butter, softened
- 1 3/4 cups granulated sugar
- 2 large eggs
- 1 teaspoon vanilla extract
- 1/2 teaspoon almond extract
- 2 cups ground almonds
- 1/2 cup all-purpose flour
- 1 teaspoon baking powder
- 1/4 teaspoon salt

Instructions

1. Preheat the oven to 350°F (175°C). Grease and flour a 9x13 inch baking pan.
2. In the bowl of a stand mixer fitted with the paddle attachment, cream together the butter and sugar until light and fluffy.
3. Add the eggs one at a time, then add the vanilla and almond extracts. Mix until well combined.
4. In a separate bowl, whisk together the ground almonds, flour, baking powder, and salt.
5. Gradually add the dry ingredients to the wet ingredients, mixing until just combined.
6. Pour the batter into the prepared pan and bake for 30-35 minutes, or until a toothpick inserted into the center comes out clean.
7. Let the cake cool completely before serving.

NUTRITIONAL FACTS
- Calories: 350
- Fat: 20 grams
- Carbohydrates: 35 grams
- Protein: 10 grams

Kladdkaka (Ooey-Gooey Chocolate Cake)

Description: Kladdkaka is a rich and decadent chocolate cake that is perfect for fika. It is made with butter, sugar, eggs, and cocoa powder, and has a gooey, fudgy texture.

Ingredients

- 1 cup (2 sticks) unsalted butter, softened
- 2 cups granulated sugar
- 2 large eggs
- 1 teaspoon vanilla extract
- 1 cup all-purpose flour
- 1/2 cup unsweetened cocoa powder
- 1/4 teaspoon salt

Instructions

1. Preheat the oven to 350°F (175°C). Grease and flour a 9x13 inch baking pan.
2. In the bowl of a stand mixer fitted with the paddle attachment, cream together the butter and sugar until light and fluffy.
3. Add the eggs one at a time, then add the vanilla extract. Mix until well combined.
4. In a separate bowl, whisk together the flour, cocoa powder, and salt.
5. Gradually add the dry ingredients to the wet ingredients, mixing until just combined.
6. Pour the batter into the prepared pan and bake for 20-25 minutes, or until a toothpick inserted into the center comes out with just a few moist crumbs attached.
7. Let the cake cool completely before serving.

NUTRITIONAL FACTS

- Calories: 400
- Fat: 25 grams
- Carbohydrates: 40 grams
- Protein: 10 grams

Semlor (Swedish Shrovetide Buns)

Description: are traditional Swedish buns that are enjoyed during Shrovetide (the week before Lent). They are made with a sweet dough that is filled with almond paste and whipped cream, and are often topped with a sprinkle of powdered sugar.

Ingredients

For the dough

- 1 cup (2 sticks) unsalted butter, softened
- 1/2 cup granulated sugar
- 1 teaspoon ground cardamom
- 1/4 teaspoon salt
- 1/2 cup warm milk (110-115°F)
- 1 packet (2 1/4 teaspoons) active dry yeast
- 2 large eggs
- 3 cups all-purpose flour, plus more for dusting

For the filling

- 1 cup almond paste
- 1/2 cup heavy cream, whipped

For the topping

- Powdered sugar

Instructions

1. In the bowl of a stand mixer fitted with the paddle attachment, cream together the butter, granulated sugar, cardamom, and salt until light and fluffy.
2. In a small bowl, whisk together the warm milk and yeast. Let stand for 5 minutes, or until the yeast is foamy.
3. Add the eggs to the butter mixture one at a time, then add the yeast mixture. Mix until well combined.
4. Gradually add the flour, 1 cup at a time, until the dough comes together and forms a ball.
5. Turn the dough out onto a lightly floured surface and knead for 5-7 minutes, or until the dough is smooth and elastic.
6. Place the dough in a lightly greased bowl, cover with plastic wrap, and let rise in a warm place for 1 hour, or until the dough has doubled in size.

7. While the dough is rising, make the filling by combining the almond paste and whipped cream in a small bowl.
8. Once the dough has risen, punch it down and turn it out onto a lightly floured surface. Roll out the dough into a rectangle that is about 12x18 inches.
9. Spread the filling evenly over the dough, leaving a 1-inch border around the edges.
10. Starting from the long side, roll up the dough tightly. Pinch the edges to seal.
11. Cut the roll into 12 equal pieces and place them on a baking sheet lined with parchment paper.
12. Cover the rolls with plastic wrap and let rise in a warm place for 30 minutes, or until the rolls have doubled in size.
13. Preheat the oven to 375°F (190°C).
14. Bake the rolls for 15-20 minutes, or until they are golden brown.
15. Let the rolls cool slightly before serving. Sprinkle it with powdered sugar before serving.

NUTRITIONAL FACTS
- Calories: 450
- Fat: 25 grams
- Carbohydrates: 50 grams
- Protein: 10 grams

Vaniljbullar (Vanilla Cardamom Buns)

Description: Vaniljbullar are traditional Swedish buns that are flavored with vanilla and cardamom. They are made with a sweet dough that is rolled in sugar and cinnamon, and are often served with a cup of coffee or tea.

Ingredients

- 1 cup (2 sticks) unsalted butter, softened
- 1/2 cup granulated sugar
- 1 teaspoon ground cardamom
- 1/4 teaspoon salt
- 1/2 cup warm milk (110-115°F)
- 1 packet (2 1/4 teaspoons) active dry yeast
- 2 large eggs
- 3 cups all-purpose flour, plus more for dusting

For the filling

- 1/2 cup granulated sugar
- 1 tablespoon ground cinnamon

Instructions

1. In the bowl of a stand mixer fitted with the paddle attachment, cream together the butter, granulated sugar, cardamom, and salt until light and fluffy.
2. In a small bowl, whisk together the warm milk and yeast. Let stand for 5 minutes, or until the yeast is foamy.
3. Add the eggs to the butter mixture one at a time, then add the yeast mixture. Mix until well combined.
4. Gradually add the flour, 1 cup at a time, until the dough comes together and forms a ball.
5. Turn the dough out onto a lightly floured surface and knead for 5-7 minutes, or until the dough is smooth and elastic.
6. Place the dough in a lightly greased bowl, cover with plastic wrap, and let rise in a warm place for 1 hour, or until the dough has doubled in size.
7. While the dough is rising, make the filling by combining the granulated sugar and cinnamon in a small bowl.
8. Once the dough has risen, punch it down and turn it out onto a lightly floured surface. Roll out the dough into a rectangle that is about 12x18 inches.

9. Spread the filling evenly over the dough, leaving a 1-inch border around the edges.
10. Starting from the long side, roll up the dough tightly. Pinch the edges to seal.
11. Cut the roll into 12 equal pieces and place them on a baking sheet lined with parchment paper.
12. Cover the rolls with plastic wrap and let rise in a warm place for 30 minutes, or until the rolls have doubled in size.
13. Preheat the oven to 375°F (190°C).
14. Bake the rolls for 15-20 minutes, or until they are golden brown.
15. Let the rolls cool slightly before serving.

NUTRITIONAL FACTS
- Calories: 300
- Fat: 15 grams
- Carbohydrates: 40 grams
- Protein: 5 grams

Prinsesstårta (Swedish Princess Cake)

Description: Prinsesstårta is a classic Swedish cake that is often served at special occasions. It is made with layers of sponge cake, raspberry jam, vanilla custard, and whipped cream, and is covered in a layer of green marzipan.

Ingredients

For the sponge cake
- 1 cup (2 sticks) unsalted butter, softened
- 1 3/4 cups granulated sugar
- 2 large eggs
- 1 teaspoon vanilla extract
- 2 1/4 cups all-purpose flour
- 1 teaspoon baking powder
- 1/2 teaspoon salt
- 1 cup milk

For the raspberry jam
- 1 (12-ounce) package frozen raspberries
- 1/2 cup granulated sugar
- 1 tablespoon lemon juice

For the vanilla custard
- 1 cup milk
- 1/4 cup granulated sugar
- 1/4 cup cornstarch
- 1/4 teaspoon salt
- 2 large egg yolks
- 1 teaspoon vanilla extract

For the whipped cream
- 1 cup heavy cream
- 1/4 cup granulated sugar

For the marzipan
- 1 (7-ounce) package marzipan
- Green food coloring

Instructions

1. Preheat the oven to 350°F (175°C). Grease and flour two 9-inch round baking pans.
2. In the bowl of a stand mixer fitted with the paddle attachment, cream together the butter and sugar until light and fluffy.
3. Add the eggs one at a time, then add the vanilla extract. Mix until well combined.
4. In a separate bowl, whisk together the flour, baking powder, and salt.
5. Gradually add the dry ingredients to the wet ingredients, alternating with the milk, beginning and ending with the dry ingredients. Mix until just combined.
6. Divide the batter between the prepared baking pans and bake for 25-30 minutes, or until a toothpick inserted into the center comes out clean.
7. Let the cakes cool completely in the pans before assembling the cake.
8. To make the raspberry jam, combine the raspberries, sugar, and lemon juice in a small saucepan. Bring to a simmer over medium heat and cook for 10-15 minutes, or until the jam has thickened.
9. To make the vanilla custard, whisk together the milk, sugar, cornstarch, and salt in a medium saucepan. Bring to a simmer over medium heat, stirring constantly. Reduce heat to low and simmer for 5-7 minutes, or until the custard has thickened.
10. Remove the custard from the heat and stir in the egg yolks. Return the saucepan to low heat and cook for 1-2 minutes, or until the custard has thickened further.
11. Remove the custard from the heat and stir in the vanilla extract. Let cool completely.
12. To make the whipped cream, beat the heavy cream and sugar together in a medium bowl until stiff peaks form.
13. To assemble the cake, place one of the cake layers on a serving plate. Spread with half of the raspberry jam. Top with half of the vanilla custard. Repeat with the remaining cake layer, raspberry jam, and vanilla custard.
14. Spread the whipped cream over the top of the cake.
15. To make the marzipan, knead the marzipan until it is soft and pliable. Add a few drops of green food coloring and knead until the color is evenly distributed.
16. Roll out the marzipan into a thin sheet and drape it over the cake. Trim the edges to fit.
17. Refrigerate the cake for at least 4 hours before serving.

NUTRITIONAL FACTS
- Calories: 500
- Fat: 25 grams
- Carbohydrates: 60 grams
- Protein: 10 grams

Mazariner (Almond Tartlets)

Description: Mazariner are traditional Swedish almond tartlets that are made with a sweet pastry dough and filled with a rich almond cream. They are often served with a cup of coffee or tea.

Ingredients

For the pastry dough
- 1 cup (2 sticks) unsalted butter, cold and cut into small pieces
- 2 1/4 cups all-purpose flour
- 1/2 cup powdered sugar
- 1 large egg yolk
- 1 tablespoon cold water

For the almond cream
- 1 cup (2 sticks) unsalted butter, softened
- 1 cup granulated sugar
- 2 large eggs
- 1 teaspoon almond extract
- 1 cup ground almonds

Instructions

1. Preheat the oven to 350°F (175°C). Grease and flour a 12-cup muffin tin.
2. In a large bowl, combine the flour, powdered sugar, and salt. Add the butter and use your fingers to work it into the flour mixture until it resembles coarse crumbs.
3. Add the egg yolk and water and mix until the dough just comes together. Do not overmix.
4. Wrap the dough in plastic wrap and refrigerate for at least 30 minutes.
5. On a lightly floured surface, roll out the dough to a thickness of 1/8 inch. Cut out 12 circles of dough and line the muffin cups with the dough.
6. In a medium bowl, cream together the butter and sugar until light and fluffy. Beat in the eggs one at a time, then stir in the almond extract. Fold in the ground almonds.
7. Spoon the almond cream into the prepared muffin cups.
8. Bake for 20-25 minutes, or until the almond cream is set and the edges of the pastry are golden brown.
9. Let the tartlets cool in the muffin tin for 10 minutes before transferring to a wire rack to cool completely.

NUTRITIONAL FACTS
- Calories: 250
- Fat: 15 grams
- Carbohydrates: 25 grams
- Protein: 5 grams

Chokladbollar (Chocolate Balls)

Description: Chokladbollar are traditional Swedish chocolate balls that are made with oats, cocoa powder, and butter. They are often rolled in powdered sugar and served with a cup of coffee or tea.

Ingredients

- 1 cup (2 sticks) unsalted butter, softened
- 1 cup granulated sugar
- 1/2 cup unsweetened cocoa powder
- 1 teaspoon vanilla extract
- 3 cups rolled oats
- 1/2 cup chopped nuts (optional)
- Powdered sugar for coating

Instructions

1. In a large bowl, cream together the butter and sugar until light and fluffy. Beat in the cocoa powder and vanilla extract.
2. Stir in the oats and chopped nuts, if desired.
3. Roll the mixture into 1-inch balls.
4. Roll the balls in powdered sugar.
5. Place the chocolate balls on a parchment paper-lined baking sheet and refrigerate for at least 30 minutes before serving.

NUTRITIONAL FACTS

- Calories: 150
- Fat: 10 grams
- Carbohydrates: 15 grams
- Protein: 5 grams

Spettekaka (Swedish Tree Cake)

Description: Spettekaka is a traditional Swedish tree cake that is made with a sweet dough that is wrapped around a spit and baked. The cake is then decorated with a variety of glazes and sprinkles.

Ingredients

For the dough

- 1 cup (2 sticks) unsalted butter, softened
- 1 cup granulated sugar
- 2 large eggs
- 1 teaspoon vanilla extract
- 3 cups all-purpose flour
- 1 teaspoon baking powder
- 1/4 teaspoon salt

For the glaze

- 1 cup powdered sugar
- 1 tablespoon milk
- 1/2 teaspoon vanilla extract

For the sprinkles

- Assorted sprinkles

Instructions

1. Preheat the oven to 350°F (175°C). Grease and flour a baking sheet.
2. In a large bowl, cream together the butter and sugar until light and fluffy. Beat in the eggs one at a time, then stir in the vanilla extract.
3. In a separate bowl, whisk together the flour, baking powder, and salt. Gradually add the dry ingredients to the wet ingredients, mixing until just combined.
4. Wrap the dough around a greased and floured spit. Place the spit on the prepared baking sheet and bake for 20-25 minutes, or until the cake is golden brown.
5. Let the cake cool slightly before glazing.
6. To make the glaze, whisk together the powdered sugar, milk, and vanilla extract. Pour the glaze over the cake and let it set for at least 30 minutes.
7. Decorate the cake with sprinkles.

NUTRITIONAL FACTS

- Calories: 250
- Fat: 10 grams
- Carbohydrates: 35 grams
- Protein: 5 grams

Toscakaka (Almond Cake with Caramel Glaze)

Description: Toscakaka is a traditional Swedish almond cake that is made with a sweet yeast dough that is topped with a layer of almonds and a caramel glaze.

Ingredients

For the dough

- 1 cup (2 sticks) unsalted butter, softened
- 1/2 cup granulated sugar
- 1 teaspoon ground cardamom
- 1/4 teaspoon salt
- 1/2 cup warm milk (110-115°F)
- 1 packet (2 1/4 teaspoons) active dry yeast
- 2 large eggs
- 3 cups all-purpose flour

For the topping

- 1 cup sliced almonds
- 1/2 cup granulated sugar
- 1/4 cup butter, melted

For the glaze

- 1 cup granulated sugar
- 1/4 cup water
- 1/4 cup heavy cream
- 1 tablespoon butter

Instructions

1. In the bowl of a stand mixer fitted with the paddle attachment, cream together the butter, sugar, cardamom, and salt until light and fluffy.
2. In a small bowl, whisk together the warm milk and yeast. Let stand for 5 minutes, or until the yeast is foamy.
3. Add the eggs to the butter mixture one at a time, then add the yeast mixture. Mix until well combined.
4. Gradually add the flour, 1 cup at a time, until the dough comes together and forms a ball.

5. Turn the dough out onto a lightly floured surface and knead for 5-7 minutes, or until the dough is smooth and elastic.
6. Place the dough in a lightly greased bowl, cover with plastic wrap, and let rise in a warm place for 1 hour, or until the dough has doubled in size.
7. Punch down the dough and turn it out onto a lightly floured surface. Roll out the dough into a rectangle that is about 12x18 inches.
8. Transfer the dough to a greased and floured baking sheet. Spread the almonds evenly over the dough.
9. In a small bowl, combine the granulated sugar and melted butter. Sprinkle the sugar mixture evenly over the almonds.
10. Bake the cake for 20-25 minutes, or until the almonds are golden brown and the cake is cooked through.
11. While the cake is baking, make the glaze. In a small saucepan, combine the granulated sugar, water, heavy cream, and butter. Bring to a simmer over medium heat, stirring constantly. Reduce heat to low and simmer for 5-7 minutes, or until the glaze has thickened.
12. Pour the glaze over the hot cake and let it cool completely.

NUTRITIONAL FACTS
- Calories: 300
- Fat: 15 grams
- Carbohydrates: 40 grams
- Protein: 5 grams

Rulltårta (Swiss Roll)

Description: Rulltårta is a traditional Swedish Swiss roll that is made with a thin layer of sponge cake that is rolled up with a sweet filling. The most popular filling is a raspberry jam, but other fillings, such as chocolate ganache or whipped cream, can also be used.

Ingredients

For the sponge cake

- 1 cup (2 sticks) unsalted butter, softened
- 1 cup granulated sugar
- 2 large eggs
- 1 teaspoon vanilla extract
- 1 cup all-purpose flour
- 1 teaspoon baking powder
- 1/4 teaspoon salt

For the filling

- 1 cup raspberry jam

Instructions:
1. Preheat the oven to 375°F (190°C). Line a 10x15 inch baking sheet with parchment paper.
2. In the bowl of a stand mixer fitted with the paddle attachment, cream together the butter and sugar until light and fluffy. Beat in the eggs one at a time, then stir in the vanilla extract.
3. In a separate bowl, whisk together the flour, baking powder, and salt. Gradually add the dry ingredients to the wet ingredients, mixing until just combined.
4. Pour the batter onto the prepared baking sheet and spread it out evenly. Bake for 10-12 minutes, or until the cake is golden brown and springs back when touched.
5. Immediately after removing the cake from the oven, sprinkle it with a little bit of granulated sugar. Place a clean tea towel over the cake and invert the cake onto the tea towel. Carefully peel off the parchment paper.
6. Spread the raspberry jam evenly over the cake. Starting from one of the short ends, roll up the cake tightly. Wrap the cake in the tea towel and let it cool completely.

NUTRITIONAL FACTS
- Calories: 250
- Fat: 10 grams
- Carbohydrates: 35 grams
- Protein: 5 grams

Dammsugare (Vacuum Cleaner Pastries)

Description: Dammsugare are traditional Swedish pastries that are made with a sweet dough that is filled with a chocolate cream and topped with a green marzipan frosting. They are often shaped like vacuum cleaners, hence their name.

Ingredients

For the dough

- 1 cup (2 sticks) unsalted butter, softened
- 1/2 cup granulated sugar
- 1 large egg
- 1 teaspoon vanilla extract
- 2 1/4 cups all-purpose flour
- 1 teaspoon baking powder
- 1/4 teaspoon salt

For the filling

- 1 cup heavy cream
- 8 ounces semisweet chocolate, chopped

For the frosting

- 1 cup marzipan
- Green food coloring

Instructions

1. In the bowl of a stand mixer fitted with the paddle attachment, cream together the butter and sugar until light and fluffy. Beat in the egg and vanilla extract.
2. In a separate bowl, whisk together the flour, baking powder, and salt. Gradually add the dry ingredients to the wet ingredients, mixing until just combined.
3. Divide the dough in half and wrap each half in plastic wrap. Refrigerate for at least 30 minutes.
4. On a lightly floured surface, roll out one half of the dough to a thickness of 1/8 inch. Cut out 12 rectangles of dough, each measuring 3x4 inches.
5. Place the rectangles of dough on a baking sheet lined with parchment paper. Bake for 10-12 minutes, or until the edges are golden brown.
6. Let the pastries cool completely.

7. To make the filling, heat the heavy cream in a small saucepan over medium heat until it is simmering. Remove the saucepan from the heat and add the chocolate. Let sit for 5 minutes, then stir until the chocolate is melted and smooth.

8. To make the frosting, knead the marzipan until it is soft and pliable. Add a few drops of green food coloring and knead until the color is evenly distributed.

9. To assemble the pastries, spread a layer of chocolate cream on one half of each pastry. Top with the other half of the pastry and press down gently.

10. Roll out the remaining half of the dough to a thickness of 1/8 inch. Cut out 12 strips of dough, each measuring 1/2x4 inches.

11. Place the strips of dough on the pastries to resemble vacuum cleaner hoses.

12. Refrigerate the pastries for at least 30 minutes before serving.

NUTRITIONAL FACTS
- Calories: 300
- Fat: 15 grams
- Carbohydrates: 40 grams
- Protein: 5 grams

Wienerbröd (Danish Pastries)

Description: Wienerbröd are traditional Swedish pastries that are made with a sweet dough that is rolled and folded several times to create a flaky texture. They are often filled with a variety of fillings, such as jam, custard, or chocolate.

Ingredients

For the dough
- 1 cup (2 sticks) unsalted butter, cold and cut into small pieces
- 2 1/4 cups all-purpose flour
- 1/2 cup granulated sugar
- 1 teaspoon salt
- 1 large egg yolk
- 1/4 cup cold water

For the filling
- 1 cup raspberry jam

Instructions

1. In the bowl of a food processor, combine the flour, sugar, and salt. Pulse to combine. Add the butter and pulse until the mixture resembles coarse crumbs.
2. Add the egg yolk and water and pulse until the dough just comes together. Do not overmix.
3. Wrap the dough in plastic wrap and refrigerate for at least 1 hour.
4. On a lightly floured surface, roll out the dough to a rectangle that is about 12x18 inches. Fold the dough in thirds, like a letter. Wrap the dough in plastic wrap and refrigerate for at least 30 minutes.
5. Repeat the rolling and folding process two more times.
6. On a lightly floured surface, roll out the dough to a rectangle that is about 12x18 inches. Cut out 12 rectangles of dough, each measuring 3x4 inches.
7. Place the rectangles of dough on a baking sheet lined with parchment paper. Spread a layer of raspberry jam on one half of each pastry. Top with the other half of the pastry and press down gently.
8. Bake the pastries for 15-20 minutes, or until they are golden brown.
9. Let the pastries cool completely before serving.

NUTRITIONAL FACTS
- Calories: 350
- Fat: 20 grams
- Carbohydrates: 45 grams
- Protein: 5 grams

Lussekatter (Saffron Buns)

Description: Lussekatter are traditional Swedish saffron buns that are made with a sweet dough that is flavored with saffron and cardamom. They are often shaped into the shape of a cat, with raisins for eyes and a tail.

Ingredients

- 1 cup (2 sticks) unsalted butter, softened
- 1/2 cup granulated sugar
- 1 teaspoon ground cardamom
- 1/4 teaspoon saffron threads, crushed
- 1/2 cup warm milk (110-115°F)
- 1 packet (2 1/4 teaspoons) active dry yeast
- 2 large eggs
- 3 cups all-purpose flour
- 1/2 cup raisins

Instructions

1. In the bowl of a stand mixer fitted with the paddle attachment, cream together the butter, sugar, cardamom, and saffron until light and fluffy.
2. In a small bowl, whisk together the warm milk and yeast. Let stand for 5 minutes, or until the yeast is foamy.
3. Add the eggs to the butter mixture one at a time, then add the yeast mixture. Mix until well combined.
4. Gradually add the flour, 1 cup at a time, until the dough comes together and forms a ball.
5. Turn the dough out onto a lightly floured surface and knead for 5-7 minutes, or until the dough is smooth and elastic.
6. Place the dough in a lightly greased bowl, cover with plastic wrap, and let rise in a warm place for 1 hour, or until the dough has doubled in size.
7. Punch down the dough and turn it out onto a lightly floured surface. Divide the dough into 12 equal pieces.
8. Roll each piece of dough into a rope that is about 12 inches long. Shape the ropes into the shape of a cat, with a head, body, tail, and legs. Place the raisins on the head for eyes and the tail for a tail.

9. Place the buns on a baking sheet lined with parchment paper. Cover with plastic wrap and let rise in a warm place for 30 minutes, or until the buns have doubled in size.
10. Preheat the oven to 375°F (190°C).
11. Bake the buns for 15-20 minutes, or until they are golden brown.
12. Let the buns cool completely before serving.

NUTRITIONAL FACTS
- Calories: 300
- Fat: 15 grams
- Carbohydrates: 40 grams
- Protein: 5 grams

Pepparkakor (Gingerbread Cookies)

Description: Pepparkakor are traditional Swedish gingerbread cookies that are made with a combination of spices, such as ginger, cinnamon, cloves, and nutmeg. They are often cut into fun shapes, such as hearts, stars, and trees, and decorated with icing or sprinkles.

Ingredients

- 1 cup (2 sticks) unsalted butter, softened
- 1 cup granulated sugar
- 1 large egg
- 1/4 cup molasses
- 2 cups all-purpose flour
- 1 teaspoon ground ginger
- 1 teaspoon ground cinnamon
- 1/2 teaspoon ground cloves
- 1/4 teaspoon ground nutmeg

Instructions

1. Preheat the oven to 350°F (175°C). Line a baking sheet with parchment paper.
2. In the bowl of a stand mixer fitted with the paddle attachment, cream together the butter and sugar until light and fluffy. Beat in the egg and molasses.
3. In a separate bowl, whisk together the flour, ginger, cinnamon, cloves, and nutmeg. Gradually add the dry ingredients to the wet ingredients, mixing until just combined.
4. Wrap the dough in plastic wrap and refrigerate for at least 30 minutes.
5. On a lightly floured surface, roll out the dough to a thickness of 1/8 inch. Cut out the dough into desired shapes using cookie cutters.
6. Place the cookies on the prepared baking sheet and bake for 10-12 minutes, or until the edges are golden brown.
7. Let the cookies cool completely before decorating.

To decorate the cookies

You can decorate the cookies with icing, sprinkles, or other edible decorations. For a simple icing, whisk together 1 cup of powdered sugar, 2 tablespoons of milk, and 1/2 teaspoon of vanilla extract. Dip the cookies in the icing and let them dry completely.

NUTRITIONAL FACTS

- Calories: 100
- Fat: 5 grams
- Carbohydrates: 15 grams
- Protein: 1 gram

Havreflarn (Oatmeal Cookies)

Description: Havreflarn are traditional Swedish oatmeal cookies that are made with a combination of oats, flour, and sugar. They are often flavored with vanilla and cinnamon, and have a crispy texture.

Ingredients

- 1 cup (2 sticks) unsalted butter, softened
- 1 cup granulated sugar
- 1 large egg
- 1 teaspoon vanilla extract
- 2 cups rolled oats
- 1 cup all-purpose flour
- 1 teaspoon ground cinnamon
- 1/2 teaspoon baking soda
- 1/4 teaspoon salt

Instructions

1. Preheat the oven to 350°F (175°C). Line a baking sheet with parchment paper.
2. In the bowl of a stand mixer fitted with the paddle attachment, cream together the butter and sugar until light and fluffy. Beat in the egg and vanilla extract.
3. In a separate bowl, whisk together the oats, flour, cinnamon, baking soda, and salt. Gradually add the dry ingredients to the wet ingredients, mixing until just combined.
4. Drop the dough by rounded tablespoons onto the prepared baking sheet, spacing them about 2 inches apart.
5. Bake for 10-12 minutes, or until the edges are golden brown.
6. Let the cookies cool completely on the baking sheet before transferring to a wire rack to cool completely.

NUTRITIONAL FACTS

- Calories: 150
- Fat: 10 grams
- Carbohydrates: 20 grams
- Protein: 3 grams

Drömmar (Coconut Macaroons)

Description: Drömmar are traditional Swedish coconut macaroons that are made with a combination of coconut, sugar, and egg whites. They have a light and airy texture, and are often flavored with vanilla or almond extract.

Ingredients

- 2 cups shredded coconut
- 1 cup granulated sugar
- 2 large egg whites
- 1 teaspoon vanilla extract
- 1/4 teaspoon almond extract (optional)

Instructions

1. Preheat the oven to 350°F (175°C). Line a baking sheet with parchment paper.
2. In a medium bowl, combine the coconut and sugar.
3. In a separate bowl, whisk together the egg whites, vanilla extract, and almond extract (if using).
4. Gradually add the egg whites to the coconut mixture, mixing until just combined.
5. Drop the dough by rounded tablespoons onto the prepared baking sheet, spacing them about 2 inches apart.
6. Bake for 15-20 minutes, or until the macaroons are golden brown.
7. Let the macaroons cool completely on the baking sheet before transferring to a wire rack to cool completely.

NUTRITIONAL FACTS

- Calories: 100
- Fat: 5 grams
- Carbohydrates: 15 grams
- Protein: 2 grams

Snickerdoodles (Swedish Spritz Cookies)

Description: Snickerdoodles are traditional Swedish spritz cookies that are made with a combination of butter, sugar, and flour. They are often flavored with cinnamon and sugar, and have a shortbread-like texture.

Ingredients

- 1 cup (2 sticks) unsalted butter, softened
- 1/2 cup granulated sugar
- 1 large egg
- 1 teaspoon vanilla extract
- 2 cups all-purpose flour
- 1/2 teaspoon baking soda
- 1/4 teaspoon salt

For the cinnamon sugar coating

- 1/2 cup granulated sugar
- 1 teaspoon ground cinnamon

Instructions

1. Preheat the oven to 375°F (190°C). Line a baking sheet with parchment paper.
2. In the bowl of a stand mixer fitted with the paddle attachment, cream together the butter and sugar until light and fluffy. Beat in the egg and vanilla extract.
3. In a separate bowl, whisk together the flour, baking soda, and salt. Gradually add the dry ingredients to the wet ingredients, mixing until just combined.
4. Fit a cookie press with a star-shaped disk. Fill the cookie press with the dough.
5. Pipe the dough onto the prepared baking sheet, spacing them about 2 inches apart.
6. In a small bowl, combine the granulated sugar and cinnamon. Roll the cookies in the cinnamon sugar mixture.
7. Bake for 10-12 minutes, or until the edges are golden brown.
8. Let the cookies cool completely on the baking sheet before transferring to a wire rack to cool completely.

NUTRITIONAL FACTS

- Calories: 120
- Fat: 6 grams
- Carbohydrates: 18 grams
- Protein: 2 grams

Kolabullar (Caramel Buns)

Description: Kolabullar are traditional Swedish caramel buns that are made with a sweet dough that is filled with a cinnamon-sugar filling and topped with a caramel glaze. They are often served with a cup of coffee or tea.

Ingredients

For the dough:
- 1 cup (2 sticks) unsalted butter, softened
- 1/2 cup granulated sugar
- 1 teaspoon ground cardamom
- 1/4 teaspoon salt
- 1/2 cup warm milk (110-115°F)
- 1 packet (2 1/4 teaspoons) active dry yeast
- 2 large eggs
- 3 cups all-purpose flour

For the filling
- 1/2 cup granulated sugar
- 1 tablespoon ground cinnamon

For the glaze:
- 1 cup granulated sugar
- 1/4 cup water
- 1/4 cup heavy cream
- 1 tablespoon butter

Instructions

1. In the bowl of a stand mixer fitted with the paddle attachment, cream together the butter, sugar, cardamom, and salt until light and fluffy.
2. In a small bowl, whisk together the warm milk and yeast. Let stand for 5 minutes, or until the yeast is foamy.
3. Add the eggs to the butter mixture one at a time, then add the yeast mixture. Mix until well combined.
4. Gradually add the flour, 1 cup at a time, until the dough comes together and forms a ball.

5. Turn the dough out onto a lightly floured surface and knead for 5-7 minutes, or until the dough is smooth and elastic.
6. Place the dough in a lightly greased bowl, cover with plastic wrap, and let rise in a warm place for 1 hour, or until the dough has doubled in size.
7. Punch down the dough and turn it out onto a lightly floured surface. Roll out the dough into a rectangle that is about 12x18 inches.
8. Sprinkle the cinnamon-sugar filling evenly over the dough, leaving a 1-inch border around the edges.
9. Starting from one of the long sides, roll up the dough tightly. Pinch the edges to seal.
10. Cut the roll into 12 equal pieces and place them on a baking sheet lined with parchment paper.
11. Cover the rolls with plastic wrap and let rise in a warm place for 30 minutes, or until the rolls have doubled in size.
12. Preheat the oven to 375°F (190°C).
13. Bake the rolls for 15-20 minutes, or until they are golden brown.
14. While the rolls are baking, make the glaze. In a small saucepan, combine the granulated sugar, water, heavy cream, and butter. Bring to a simmer over medium heat, stirring constantly. Reduce heat to low and simmer for 5-7 minutes, or until the glaze has thickened.
15. Pour the glaze over the hot rolls and let it cool completely.

NUTRITIONAL FACTS
- Calories: 350
- Fat: 15 grams
- Carbohydrates: 50 grams
- Protein: 5 grams

Kardemummabullar (Cardamom Buns)

Description: Kardemummabullar are traditional Swedish cardamom buns that are made with a sweet dough that is flavored with cardamom and topped with a pearl sugar. They are often served with a cup of coffee or tea.

Ingredients

- 1 cup (2 sticks) unsalted butter, softened
- 1/2 cup granulated sugar
- 1 teaspoon ground cardamom
- 1/4 teaspoon salt
- 1/2 cup warm milk (110-115°F)
- 1 packet (2 1/4 teaspoons) active dry yeast
- 2 large eggs
- 3 cups all-purpose flour

For the topping

- 1 egg, beaten
- Pearl sugar

Instructions

1. In the bowl of a stand mixer fitted with the paddle attachment, cream together the butter, sugar, cardamom, and salt until light and fluffy.
2. In a small bowl, whisk together the warm milk and yeast. Let stand for 5 minutes, or until the yeast is foamy.
3. Add the eggs to the butter mixture one at a time, then add the yeast mixture. Mix until well combined.
4. Gradually add the flour, 1 cup at a time, until the dough comes together and forms a ball.
5. Turn the dough out onto a lightly floured surface and knead for 5-7 minutes, or until the dough is smooth and elastic.
6. Place the dough in a lightly greased bowl, cover with plastic wrap, and let rise in a warm place for 1 hour, or until the dough has doubled in size.
7. Punch down the dough and turn it out onto a lightly floured surface. Divide the dough into 12 equal pieces.
8. Roll each piece of dough into a ball and place them on a baking sheet lined with parchment paper.

9. Cover the rolls with plastic wrap and let rise in a warm place for 30 minutes, or until the rolls have doubled in size.
10. Preheat the oven to 375°F (190°C).
11. Brush the rolls with the beaten egg and sprinkle with pearl sugar.
12. Bake for 15-20 minutes, or until the rolls are golden brown.
13. Let the rolls cool completely before serving.

NUTRITIONAL FACTS
- Calories: 300
- Fat: 10 grams
- Carbohydrates: 45 grams
- Protein: 5 grams

Chokladbollskaka (Chocolate Ball Cake)

Description: Chokladboll Kaka is a no-bake cake made with chocolate, oats, and butter. It is often rolled into balls and coated in chocolate sprinkles.

Ingredients

- 1 cup (120g) quick-cooking oats
- 1 cup (120g) semisweet chocolate chips
- 1/2 cup (1 stick) unsalted butter, melted
- 1/4 cup (60ml) milk
- 1/4 cup (50g) powdered sugar
- 1 tablespoon (15ml) vanilla extract
- Chocolate sprinkles, for coating

Instructions

1. In a large bowl, combine the oats, chocolate chips, melted butter, milk, powdered sugar, and vanilla extract.
2. Mix until well combined.
3. Roll the mixture into 1-inch balls.
4. Place the balls on a parchment paper-lined baking sheet.
5. Refrigerate for at least 30 minutes, or until firm.
6. Roll the balls in chocolate sprinkles.
7. Serve and enjoy!

NUTRITIONAL FACTS

- Calories: 150
- Fat: 7g
- Carbohydrates: 20g
- Protein: 2g

Äppelpaj (Apple Pie)

Description: Äppelpaj is a classic Swedish dessert made with apples, cinnamon, and sugar. It is often served with vanilla ice cream or whipped cream.

Ingredients

- 1 cup (120g) all-purpose flour
- 1/2 cup (100g) sugar
- 1/2 teaspoon (2.5g) baking powder
- 1/4 teaspoon (1.25g) salt
- 1/2 cup (1 stick) unsalted butter, cold and cut into small pieces
- 1/4 cup (60ml) ice water
- 6 cups (750g) peeled and sliced apples
- 1 cup (200g) sugar
- 1 tablespoon (15ml) ground cinnamon

Instructions

1. Preheat the oven to 375°F (190°C).
2. In a large bowl, whisk together the flour, sugar, baking powder, and salt.
3. Use your fingers to work the butter into the flour mixture until it resembles coarse crumbs.
4. Add the ice water and mix until the dough just comes together.
5. Form the dough into a ball, wrap it in plastic wrap, and refrigerate for at least 30 minutes.
6. On a lightly floured surface, roll out the dough to a 12-inch (30cm) circle.
7. Transfer the dough to a 9-inch (23cm) pie plate and trim the edges.
8. In a large bowl, combine the apples, sugar, and cinnamon.
9. Pour the apple mixture into the pie crust.
10. Roll out the remaining dough to an 11-inch (28cm) circle.
11. Place the dough over the apples and trim the edges.
12. Crimp the edges to seal.
13. Bake for 45-50 minutes, or until the crust is golden brown and the apples are tender.
14. Let cool for at least 30 minutes before serving.

NUTRITIONAL FACTS
- Calories: 300
- Fat: 10g
- Carbohydrates: 45g
- Protein: 2g

Blåbärspaj (Blueberry Pie)

Description: Blåbärpaj is a variation on apple pie made with blueberries. It is also often served with vanilla ice cream or whipped cream.

Ingredients

- 1 cup (120g) all-purpose flour
- 1/2 cup (100g) sugar
- 1/2 teaspoon (2.5g) baking powder
- 1/4 teaspoon (1.25g) salt
- 1/2 cup (1 stick) unsalted butter, cold and cut into small pieces
- 1/4 cup (60ml) ice water
- 4 cups (500g) blueberries
- 1 cup (200g) sugar
- 1 tablespoon (15ml) ground cinnamon

Instructions

1. Preheat the oven to 375°F (190°C).
2. In a large bowl, whisk together the flour, sugar, baking powder, and salt.
3. Use your fingers to work the butter into the flour mixture until it resembles coarse crumbs.
4. Add the ice water and mix until the dough just comes together.
5. Form the dough into a ball, wrap it in plastic wrap, and refrigerate for at least 30 minutes.
6. On a lightly floured surface, roll out the dough to a 12-inch (30cm) circle.
7. Transfer the dough to a 9-inch (23cm) pie plate and trim the edges.
8. In a large bowl, combine the blueberries, sugar, and cinnamon.
9. Pour the blueberry mixture into the pie crust.
10. Roll out the remaining dough to an 11-inch (28cm) circle.
11. Place the dough over the blueberries and trim the edges.
12. Crimp the edges to seal.
13. Bake for 45-50 minutes, or until the crust is golden brown and the blueberries are bubbling.
14. Let cool for at least 30 minutes before serving.

NUTRITIONAL FACTS

- Calories: 300
- Fat: 10g
- Carbohydrates: 45g
- Protein: 2g

Rabarberpaj (Rhubarb Pie)

Description: Rabarberpaj is a pie made with rhubarb, sugar, and flour. It is often served with vanilla ice cream or whipped cream.

Ingredients

- 1 cup (120g) all-purpose flour
- 1/2 cup (100g) sugar
- 1/2 teaspoon (2.5g) baking powder
- 1/4 teaspoon (1.25g) salt
- 1/2 cup (1 stick) unsalted butter, cold and cut into small pieces
- 1/4 cup (60ml) ice water
- 4 cups (500g) rhubarb, cut into 1-inch (2.5cm) pieces
- 1 cup (200g) sugar
- 1 tablespoon (15ml) ground cinnamon

Instructions

1. Preheat the oven to 375°F (190°C).
2. In a large bowl, whisk together the flour, sugar, baking powder, and salt.
3. Use your fingers to work the butter into the flour mixture until it resembles coarse crumbs.
4. Add the ice water and mix until the dough just comes together.
5. Form the dough into a ball, wrap it in plastic wrap, and refrigerate for at least 30 minutes.
6. On a lightly floured surface, roll out the dough to a 12-inch (30cm) circle.
7. Transfer the dough to a 9-inch (23cm) pie plate and trim the edges.
8. In a large bowl, combine the rhubarb, sugar, and cinnamon.
9. Pour the rhubarb mixture into the pie crust.
10. Roll out the remaining dough to an 11-inch (28cm) circle.
11. Place the dough over the rhubarb and trim the edges.
12. Crimp the edges to seal.
13. Bake for 45-50 minutes, or until the crust is golden brown and the rhubarb is tender.
14. Let cool for at least 30 minutes before serving.

NUTRITIONAL FACTS

- Calories: 300
- Fat: 10g
- Carbohydrates: 45g
- Protein: 2g

Krusbärspaj (Gooseberry Pie)

Description: Krusbärspaj is a pie made with gooseberries, sugar, and flour. It is often served with vanilla ice cream or whipped cream.

Ingredients

- 1 cup (120g) all-purpose flour
- 1/2 cup (100g) sugar
- 1/2 teaspoon (2.5g) baking powder
- 1/4 teaspoon (1.25g) salt
- 1/2 cup (1 stick) unsalted butter, cold and cut into small pieces
- 1/4 cup (60ml) ice water
- 4 cups (500g) gooseberries
- 1 cup (200g) sugar
- 1 tablespoon (15ml) ground cinnamon

Instructions

1. Preheat the oven to 375°F (190°C).
2. In a large bowl, whisk together the flour, sugar, baking powder, and salt.
3. Use your fingers to work the butter into the flour mixture until it resembles coarse crumbs.
4. Add the ice water and mix until the dough just comes together.
5. Form the dough into a ball, wrap it in plastic wrap, and refrigerate for at least 30 minutes.
6. On a lightly floured surface, roll out the dough to a 12-inch (30cm) circle.
7. Transfer the dough to a 9-inch (23cm) pie plate and trim the edges.
8. In a large bowl, combine the gooseberries, sugar, and cinnamon.
9. Pour the gooseberry mixture into the pie crust.
10. Roll out the remaining dough to an 11-inch (28cm) circle.
11. Place the dough over the gooseberries and trim the edges.
12. Crimp the edges to seal.
13. Bake for 45-50 minutes, or until the crust is golden brown and the gooseberries are tender.
14. Let cool for at least 30 minutes before serving.

NUTRITIONAL FACTS

- Calories: 300
- Fat: 10g
- Carbohydrates: 45g
- Protein: 2g

Lingonberry Pie

Description: Lingonberry pie is a pie made with lingonberries, sugar, and flour. It is often served with vanilla ice cream or whipped cream.

Ingredients

- 1 cup (120g) all-purpose flour
- 1/2 cup (100g) sugar
- 1/2 teaspoon (2.5g) baking powder
- 1/4 teaspoon (1.25g) salt
- 1/2 cup (1 stick) unsalted butter, cold and cut into small pieces
- 1/4 cup (60ml) ice water
- 4 cups (500g) lingonberries
- 1 cup (200g) sugar
- 1 tablespoon (15ml) ground cinnamon

Instructions

1. Preheat the oven to 375°F (190°C).
2. In a large bowl, whisk together the flour, sugar, baking powder, and salt.
3. Use your fingers to work the butter into the flour mixture until it resembles coarse crumbs.
4. Add the ice water and mix until the dough just comes together.
5. Form the dough into a ball, wrap it in plastic wrap, and refrigerate for at least 30 minutes.
6. On a lightly floured surface, roll out the dough to a 12-inch (30cm) circle.
7. Transfer the dough to a 9-inch (23cm) pie plate and trim the edges.
8. In a large bowl, combine the lingonberries, sugar, and cinnamon.
9. Pour the lingonberry mixture into the pie crust.
10. Roll out the remaining dough to an 11-inch (28cm) circle.
11. Place the dough over the lingonberries and trim the edges.
12. Crimp the edges to seal.
13. Bake for 45-50 minutes, or until the crust is golden brown and the lingonberries are bubbling.
14. Let cool for at least 30 minutes before serving.

NUTRITIONAL FACTS

- Calories: 300
- Fat: 10g
- Carbohydrates: 45g
- Protein: 2g

Smulpaj (Crumble Pie)

Description: Smulpaj is a pie made with fruit, sugar, and flour. The topping is made with oats, butter, and sugar. It is often served with vanilla ice cream or whipped cream.

Ingredients

For the filling:

- 4 cups (500g) fruit (such as apples, blueberries, or raspberries)
- 1 cup (200g) sugar
- 1 tablespoon (15ml) ground cinnamon
- For the topping:
- 1 cup (120g) all-purpose flour
- 1/2 cup (100g) sugar
- 1/2 cup (1 stick) unsalted butter, cold and cut into small pieces
- 1/2 cup (50g) oats

Instructions

1. Preheat the oven to 375°F (190°C).
2. In a large bowl, combine the fruit, sugar, and cinnamon.
3. Pour the fruit mixture into a 9-inch (23cm) pie plate.
4. In a medium bowl, combine the flour, sugar, butter, and oats.
5. Use your fingers to work the ingredients together until the mixture resembles coarse crumbs.
6. Sprinkle the crumb topping over the fruit.
7. Bake for 45-50 minutes, or until the crust is golden brown and the fruit is bubbling.
8. Let cool for at least 30 minutes before serving.

NUTRITIONAL FACTS

- Calories: 300
- Fat: 10g
- Carbohydrates: 45g
- Protein: 2g

CHAPTER 3:SAVORY BITES

Smörgåstårta (Swedish Sandwich Cake)

Description: Smörgåstårta is a Swedish sandwich cake made with layers of bread, fillings, and toppings. It is often served at parties and celebrations.

Ingredients

For the bread layers:
- 1 loaf (500g) white bread, thinly sliced

For the fillings
- 1 can (400g) tuna, drained
- 1/2 cup (100g) mayonnaise
- 1/4 cup (50g) chopped red onion
- 1/4 cup (50g) chopped dill
- 1/2 cup (100g) shrimp, cooked and chopped
- 1/2 cup (100g) hard-boiled eggs, chopped
- 1/2 cup (100g) grated cheese

For the topping
- 1/2 cup (100g) mayonnaise
- 1/4 cup (50g) sour cream
- 1 tablespoon (15ml) lemon juice
- 1/4 cup (50g) chopped fresh parsley

Instructions

1. To make the bread layers, use a cookie cutter to cut circles out of the bread slices.
2. To make the tuna filling, combine the tuna, mayonnaise, red onion, and dill in a bowl. Season with salt and pepper to taste.
3. To make the shrimp filling, combine the shrimp, mayonnaise, hard-boiled eggs, and cheese in a bowl. Season with salt and pepper to taste.
4. To assemble the sandwich cake, place a layer of bread circles on a serving plate. Spread with the tuna filling. Repeat with another layer of bread circles and the shrimp filling. Top with a final layer of bread circles.

5. To make the topping, combine the mayonnaise, sour cream, lemon juice, and parsley in a bowl. Spread the topping over the sandwich cake.
6. Refrigerate for at least 4 hours before serving.

NUTRITIONAL FACTS
- Calories: 300
- Fat: 15g
- Carbohydrates: 30g
- Protein: 15g

Kötbullar (Swedish Meatballs)

Description: Kötbullar are Swedish meatballs made with ground beef, pork, and spices. They are often served with mashed potatoes, gravy, and lingonberry jam.

Ingredients

- 1 pound (500g) ground beef
- 1 pound (500g) ground pork
- 1 onion, finely chopped
- 1 egg, beaten
- 1/2 cup (100g) bread crumbs
- 1/4 cup (50ml) milk
- 1 teaspoon (5g) salt
- 1/2 teaspoon (2.5g) black pepper
- 1/4 teaspoon (1.25g) ground nutmeg

Instructions

1. In a large bowl, combine the ground beef, ground pork, onion, egg, bread crumbs, milk, salt, pepper, and nutmeg. Mix well.
2. Form the meat mixture into 1-inch (2.5cm) meatballs.
3. Heat a large skillet over medium heat. Add the meatballs and cook until browned on all sides.
4. Transfer the meatballs to a baking dish.
5. Bake at 375°F (190°C) for 20-25 minutes, or until cooked through.
6. Serve with mashed potatoes, gravy, and lingonberry jam.

NUTRITIONAL FACTS
- Calories: 100
- Fat: 5g
- Carbohydrates: 10g
- Protein: 10g

Gravad Lax (Cured Salmon)

Description: Gravad lax is a Swedish cured salmon dish made with dill, sugar, and salt. It is often served as an appetizer or main course.

Ingredients

- 1 side (1.5-2 pounds) salmon filet, skin on
- 1/2 cup (100g) sugar
- 1/2 cup (100g) salt
- 1 tablespoon (15ml) chopped fresh dill

Instructions

1. In a small bowl, combine the sugar, salt, and dill.
2. Place the salmon filet in a non-reactive dish. Sprinkle the sugar mixture over the salmon, making sure to cover all surfaces.
3. Wrap the salmon tightly in plastic wrap and refrigerate for 24-48 hours.
4. When the salmon is cured, rinse it off under cold water and pat it dry.
5. Slice the salmon thinly and serve with bread, crackers, or potatoes.

NUTRITIONAL FACTS

- Calories: 200
- Fat: 10g
- Carbohydrates: 0g
- Protein: 20g

Janssons Frestelse (Anchovy Potato Casserole)

Description: Janssons Frestelse is a Swedish anchovy potato casserole made with potatoes, anchovies, onions, and cream. It is often served as a side dish or main course.

Ingredients

- 2 pounds (1kg) potatoes, thinly sliced
- 1 can (120g) anchovies, drained and chopped
- 1 onion, finely chopped
- 2 cups (500ml) heavy cream
- 1/2 cup (100g) grated Parmesan cheese
- Salt and pepper to taste

Instructions

1. Preheat the oven to 375°F (190°C).
2. In a large bowl, combine the potatoes, anchovies, onion, heavy cream, Parmesan cheese, salt, and pepper. Mix well.
3. Pour the potato mixture into a 9x13 inch (23x33cm) baking dish.
4. Bake for 45-50 minutes, or until the potatoes are tender and the casserole is bubbly and golden brown.
5. Serve hot.

NUTRITIONAL FACTS

- Calories: 300
- Fat: 15g
- Carbohydrates: 30g
- Protein: 10g

Husmanskost (Traditional Swedish Fare)

Description: Husmanskost is a traditional Swedish fare that typically consists of simple, hearty dishes made with local ingredients. Some common dishes include:

- Köttbullar: Swedish meatballs
- Korv stroganoff: Sausage stroganoff
- Pannkakor: Swedish pancakes
- Potato pancakes
- Blood pudding
- Grönkålssoppa: Kale soup
- Husmanskost: Traditional Swedish fare

Ingredients

The ingredients for dishes vary depending on the specific dish being made. However, some common ingredients include:

Potatoes

- Meat (beef, pork, chicken, fish)
- Bread
- Dairy products (milk, cheese, butter)
- Vegetables (cabbage, carrots, onions)

Instructions

The preparation instructions for dishes also vary depending on the specific dish being made. However, some general tips include:

Use fresh, local ingredients whenever possible.
Cook dishes slowly and gently to allow the flavors to develop.
Don't be afraid to experiment with different ingredients and recipes.

NUTRITIONAL FACTS

The nutritional facts for dishes vary depending on the specific dish being made. However, in general, dishes are hearty and filling, and they provide a good balance of protein, carbohydrates, and fat.

Sill (Pickled Herring)

Description: Sill is a pickled herring dish that is popular in Sweden. It is typically served as an appetizer or side dish.

Ingredients

- 1 pound (500g) herring filets
- 1 cup (250ml) vinegar
- 1 cup (250ml) water
- 1/2 cup (100g) sugar
- 1 tablespoon (15ml) salt
- 1 teaspoon (5g) black peppercorns
- 1 bay leaf
- 1 onion, sliced
- 1 carrot, sliced

Instructions

1. In a large bowl, combine the vinegar, water, sugar, salt, peppercorns, bay leaf, onion, and carrot.
2. Add the herring filets to the bowl and make sure they are completely submerged in the liquid.
3. Cover the bowl and refrigerate for at least 24 hours, or up to 3 days.
4. When the herring is pickled, serve it with bread, crackers, or potatoes.

NUTRITIONAL FACTS

- Calories: 150
- Fat: 10g
- Carbohydrates: 10g
- Protein: 15g

Räkmacka (Shrimp Sandwich)

Description: Räkmacka is a Swedish shrimp sandwich that is typically served on rye bread. It is a popular lunch or snack item.

Ingredients

- 1 loaf (500g) rye bread
- 1 pound (500g) cooked shrimp
- 1/2 cup (100g) mayonnaise
- 1/4 cup (50g) chopped red onion
- 1/4 cup (50g) chopped fresh dill
- Lemon wedges, for serving

Instructions

1. Slice the rye bread into thin slices.
2. In a bowl, combine the shrimp, mayonnaise, red onion, and dill.
3. Spread the shrimp mixture on the bread slices.
4. Serve immediately, garnished with lemon wedges.

NUTRITIONAL FACTS

- Calories: 300
- Fat: 15g
- Carbohydrates: 30g
- Protein: 20g

Äggsmörgås (Egg Sandwich)

Description: Äggsmörgås is a Swedish egg sandwich that is typically served on rye bread. It is a popular breakfast or lunch item.

Ingredients

- 1 loaf (500g) rye bread
- 6 eggs
- 1/2 cup (100g) mayonnaise
- 1/4 cup (50g) chopped red onion
- 1/4 cup (50g) chopped fresh dill
- Salt and pepper to taste

Instructions

1. Slice the rye bread into thin slices.
2. In a bowl, whisk together the eggs, mayonnaise, red onion, dill, salt, and pepper.
3. Heat a large skillet over medium heat. Add the egg mixture and cook until set.
4. Spread the egg mixture on the bread slices.
5. Serve immediately.

NUTRITIONAL FACTS
- Calories: 300
- Fat: 15g
- Carbohydrates: 30g
- Protein: 20g

Tunnbrödsrulle (Swedish Wrap)

Description: Tunnbrödsrulle is a Swedish wrap that is made with a thin, flatbread called tunnbröd. It is typically filled with meat, cheese, and vegetables.

Ingredients

- 1 package (10) tunnbröd flatbreads
- 1 pound (500g) thinly sliced meat (such as ham, roast beef, or turkey)
- 1 cup (200g) shredded cheese (such as cheddar, mozzarella, or Swiss)
- 1 cup (100g) chopped vegetables (such as lettuce, tomatoes, onions, or cucumbers)
- Mustard, mayonnaise, or other condiments, to taste

Instructions

1. Spread a thin layer of mustard, mayonnaise, or other condiments on a tunnbröd flatbread.
2. Top with the meat, cheese, and vegetables.
3. Roll up the flatbread tightly.
4. Serve immediately or wrap in plastic wrap and refrigerate for later.

NUTRITIONAL FACTS

- Calories: 350
- Fat: 15g
- Carbohydrates: 40g
- Protein: 25g

Pitepalt (Potato Dumplings)

Description: Pitepalt is a Swedish potato dumpling dish that is typically served with lingonberry jam. It is a popular dish in the northern part of Sweden.

Ingredients

- 2 pounds (1kg) potatoes, peeled and grated
- 1/2 cup (100g) all-purpose flour
- 1/4 cup (50g) chopped onion
- 1 egg
- 1 teaspoon (5g) salt
- 1/2 teaspoon (2.5g) black pepper
- Lingonberry jam, for serving

Instructions

1. In a large bowl, combine the potatoes, flour, onion, egg, salt, and pepper. Mix well.
2. Form the mixture into small dumplings.
3. Bring a large pot of salted water to a boil. Add the dumplings and cook for 20-25 minutes, or until they are cooked through.
4. Serve the dumplings with lingonberry jam.

NUTRITIONAL FACTS

- Calories: 200
- Fat: 5g
- Carbohydrates: 30g
- Protein: 10g

Kroppkakor (Boiled Potato Dumplings)

Description: Kroppkakor are boiled potato dumplings that are typically filled with pork and bacon. They are a popular dish in the southern part of Sweden.

Ingredients

For the dough:
- 2 pounds (1kg) potatoes, peeled and grated
- 1/2 cup (100g) all-purpose flour
- 1 egg
- 1 teaspoon (5g) salt

For the filling:
- 1 pound (500g) ground pork
- 1/2 pound (250g) bacon, chopped
- 1 onion, chopped
- 1/2 teaspoon (2.5g) salt
- 1/4 teaspoon (1.25g) black pepper

Instructions

1. To make the dough, combine the potatoes, flour, egg, and salt in a large bowl. Mix well.
2. To make the filling, combine the pork, bacon, onion, salt, and pepper in a bowl. Mix well.
3. To assemble the dumplings, take a handful of dough and flatten it into a circle. Place a spoonful of filling in the center of the circle. Fold the dough over the filling and pinch the edges to seal.
4. Bring a large pot of salted water to a boil. Add the dumplings and cook for 20-25 minutes, or until they are cooked through.
5. Serve the dumplings with melted butter and lingonberry jam.

NUTRITIONAL FACTS
- Calories: 250
- Fat: 10g
- Carbohydrates: 30g
- Protein: 15g

Raggmunk (Potato Pancakes)

Description: Raggmunk are potato pancakes that are made with grated potatoes, flour, and eggs. They are a popular dish in Sweden and are often served with lingonberry jam.

Ingredients

- 2 pounds (1kg) potatoes, peeled and grated
- 1/2 cup (100g) all-purpose flour
- 2 eggs
- 1/2 teaspoon (2.5g) salt
- 1/4 teaspoon (1.25g) black pepper
- Vegetable oil, for frying

Instructions

1. In a large bowl, combine the potatoes, flour, eggs, salt, and pepper. Mix well.
2. Heat a large skillet over medium heat. Add a little vegetable oil to the skillet.
3. Drop spoonfuls of the potato mixture into the skillet and flatten them into pancakes.
4. Cook the pancakes for 2-3 minutes per side, or until they are golden brown and cooked through.
5. Serve the pancakes with lingonberry jam.

NUTRITIONAL FACTS
- Calories: 200
- Fat: 10g
- Carbohydrates: 25g
- Protein: 10g

Isterband (Swedish Sausage)

Description: Isterband is a Swedish sausage that is made with pork, beef, and spices. It is a popular dish in Sweden and is often served with mashed potatoes and gravy.

Ingredients

- 1 pound (500g) ground pork
- 1 pound (500g) ground beef
- 1 onion, chopped
- 1/2 cup (100g) bread crumbs
- 1 egg
- 1 teaspoon (5g) salt
- 1/2 teaspoon (2.5g) black pepper
- 1/4 teaspoon (1.25g) ground nutmeg

Instructions

1. In a large bowl, combine the pork, beef, onion, bread crumbs, egg, salt, pepper, and nutmeg. Mix well.
2. Form the sausage mixture into a loaf.
3. Place the sausage loaf on a baking sheet and bake at 375°F (190°C) for 45-50 minutes, or until cooked through.
4. Serve the sausage with mashed potatoes and gravy.

NUTRITIONAL FACTS

- Calories: 300
- Fat: 15g
- Carbohydrates: 25g
- Protein: 20g

Blodpudding (Blood Pudding)

Description: Blodpudding is a Swedish blood pudding that is made with pork blood, oatmeal, and spices. It is a popular dish in Sweden and is often served with mashed potatoes and gravy.

Ingredients

- 1 pound (500g) pork blood
- 1 cup (200g) oatmeal
- 1 onion, chopped
- 1/2 cup (100g) bread crumbs
- 1 egg
- 1 teaspoon (5g) salt
- 1/2 teaspoon (2.5g) black pepper
- 1/4 teaspoon (1.25g) ground nutmeg

Instructions

1. In a large bowl, combine the pork blood, oatmeal, onion, bread crumbs, egg, salt, pepper, and nutmeg. Mix well.
2. Pour the mixture into a greased 9x13 inch (23x33cm) baking dish.
3. Bake at 375°F (190°C) for 45-50 minutes, or until cooked through.
4. Serve the blood pudding with mashed potatoes and gravy.

NUTRITIONAL FACTS
- Calories: 250
- Fat: 10g
- Carbohydrates: 30g
- Protein: 15g

Leverpastej (Liver Pâté)

Description: Leverpastej is a Swedish liver pâté that is made with pork liver, bacon, and spices. It is a popular dish in Sweden and is often served on bread or crackers.

Ingredients

- 1 pound (500g) pork liver
- 1/2 pound (250g) bacon, chopped
- 1 onion, chopped
- 1/2 cup (100g) bread crumbs
- 1 egg
- 1 teaspoon (5g) salt
- 1/2 teaspoon (2.5g) black pepper
- 1/4 teaspoon (1.25g) ground nutmeg

Instructions

1. In a large bowl, combine the pork liver, bacon, onion, bread crumbs, egg, salt, pepper, and nutmeg. Mix well.
2. Form the pâté mixture into a loaf.
3. Place the pâté loaf on a baking sheet and bake at 375°F (190°C) for 45-50 minutes, or until cooked through.
4. Serve the pâté on bread or crackers.

NUTRITIONAL FACTS

- ☐ Calories: 250
- ☐ Fat: 15g
- ☐ Carbohydrates: 20g
- ☐ Protein: 20g

Falukorv (Swedish Sausage)

Description: Falukorv is a Swedish sausage that is made with pork, beef, and spices. It is a popular dish in Sweden and is often served with mashed potatoes and gravy.

Ingredients

- 1 pound (500g) ground pork
- 1 pound (500g) ground beef
- 1 onion, chopped
- 1/2 cup (100g) bread crumbs
- 1 egg
- 1 teaspoon (5g) salt
- 1/2 teaspoon (2.5g) black pepper
- 1/4 teaspoon (1.25g) ground nutmeg

Instructions

1. In a large bowl, combine the pork, beef, onion, bread crumbs, egg, salt, pepper, and nutmeg. Mix well.
2. Form the sausage mixture into a loaf.
3. Place the sausage loaf on a baking sheet and bake at 375°F (190°C) for 45-50 minutes, or until cooked through.
4. Serve the sausage with mashed potatoes and gravy.

NUTRITIONAL FACTS
- Calories: 300
- Fat: 15g
- Carbohydrates: 25g
- Protein: 20g

Surkål (Sauerkraut)

Description: Surkål is a Swedish sauerkraut that is made with cabbage, salt, and water. It is a popular dish in Sweden and is often served with pork or sausage.

Ingredients
- 1 head of cabbage, finely shredded
- 1 tablespoon (15g) salt
- 1 cup (250ml) water

Instructions
1. In a large bowl, combine the cabbage, salt, and water. Mix well.
2. Transfer the mixture to a clean glass jar.
3. Cover the jar with a lid and let it ferment at room temperature for 2-3 weeks.
4. Once the sauerkraut is fermented, store it in the refrigerator.

NUTRITIONAL FACTS
- Calories: 20
- Fat: 0g
- Carbohydrates: 5g
- Protein: 1g

Rödbetssallad (Beetroot Salad)

Description: Rödbetssallad is a Swedish beetroot salad that is made with beets, vinegar, and sugar. It is a popular dish in Sweden and is often served as a side dish.

Ingredients
- 1 pound (500g) beets, cooked and peeled
- 1/2 cup (100ml) vinegar
- 1/2 cup (100g) sugar
- 1 teaspoon (5g) salt

Instructions
1. In a large bowl, combine the beets, vinegar, sugar, and salt. Mix well.
2. Cover the bowl and refrigerate for at least 2 hours before serving.

NUTRITIONAL FACTS
- Calories: 100
- Fat: 0g
- Carbohydrates: 25g
- Protein: 2g

Potatissallad (Potato Salad)

Description: Potatissallad is a Swedish potato salad that is made with potatoes, mayonnaise, and vegetables. It is a popular dish in Sweden and is often served as a side dish.

Ingredients

- 2 pounds (1kg) potatoes, cooked and peeled
- 1 cup (200g) mayonnaise
- 1/2 cup (100g) chopped celery
- 1/2 cup (100g) chopped onion
- 1/2 cup (100g) chopped carrots
- 1 teaspoon (5g) salt
- 1/2 teaspoon (2.5g) black pepper

Instructions

1. In a large bowl, combine the potatoes, mayonnaise, celery, onion, carrots, salt, and pepper. Mix well.
2. Cover the bowl and refrigerate for at least 2 hours before serving.

NUTRITIONAL FACTS

- Calories: 250
- Fat: 15g
- Carbohydrates: 30g
- Protein: 10g

CHAPTER 4: BEVERAGES

Fika Coffee

Description: Fika is a Swedish social custom that involves taking a break to enjoy coffee and pastries with friends or colleagues. It is an important part of Swedish culture and is often seen as a way to relax and socialize.

Ingredients
- 1 cup (250ml) strong coffee
- Milk or cream, to taste
- Sugar, to taste

Instructions

1. Brew a cup of strong coffee.
2. Add milk or cream and sugar to taste.
3. Enjoy!

NUTRITIONAL FACTS
- Calories: 100
- Fat: 5g
- Carbohydrates: 15g
- Protein: 5g

Tea

Description: Tea is a popular beverage in Sweden and is often served with fika. There are many different types of tea available, so you can choose your favorite.

Ingredients
- 1 tea bag
- 1 cup (250ml) boiling water

Instructions
1. Place the tea bag in a cup.
2. Pour boiling water over the tea bag.
3. Steep for 3-5 minutes, or to your desired strength.
4. Remove the tea bag and enjoy!

NUTRITIONAL FACTS
- Calories: 0
- Fat: 0g
- Carbohydrates: 0g
- Protein: 0g

Glögg (Mulled Wine)

Description: Glögg is a Swedish mulled wine that is traditionally served during the Christmas season. It is made with red wine, spices, and sugar.

Ingredients

- 1 bottle (750ml) red wine
- 1 cup (200g) sugar
- 1 cinnamon stick
- 10 cardamom pods
- 10 cloves
- 1/2 teaspoon (2.5g) ground ginger
- 1/4 teaspoon (1.25g) ground nutmeg
- Orange peel, to taste

Instructions

1. In a large saucepan, combine the red wine, sugar, cinnamon stick, cardamom pods, cloves, ginger, nutmeg, and orange peel.
2. Bring to a simmer over medium heat, stirring occasionally to dissolve the sugar.
3. Reduce heat to low and simmer for 30 minutes, or until the glögg is fragrant and flavorful.
4. Strain the glögg into a clean saucepan and serve hot.

NUTRITIONAL FACTS

- Calories: 200
- Fat: 0g
- Carbohydrates: 30g
- Protein: 0g

Julmust (Swedish Christmas Soda)

Description: Julmust is a Swedish Christmas soda that is popular during the holiday season. It is a dark, sweet soda with a unique flavor.

Ingredients

- 1 liter (34 ounces) water
- 1 cup (200g) sugar
- 1 tablespoon (15ml) brown food coloring
- 1 teaspoon (5g) vanilla extract
- 1 teaspoon (5g) cinnamon extract
- 1/2 teaspoon (2.5g) cardamom extract

Instructions

1. In a large saucepan, combine the water and sugar.
2. Bring to a boil over medium heat, stirring occasionally to dissolve the sugar.
3. Remove from heat and stir in the brown food coloring, vanilla extract, cinnamon extract, and cardamom extract.
4. Let cool completely.
5. Pour the julmust into a clean glass bottle and refrigerate for at least 24 hours before serving.

NUTRITIONAL FACTS

- Calories: 150
- Fat: 0g
- Carbohydrates: 40g
- Protein: 0g

Lingonberry Juice

Description: Lingonberry juice is a tart and refreshing juice that is made from lingonberries. It is a popular drink in Sweden and is often served with meals.

Ingredients

- 1 pound (500g) lingonberries
- 1 cup (200g) sugar
- 1 cup (250ml) water

Instructions

1. In a large saucepan, combine the lingonberries, sugar, and water.
2. Bring to a boil over medium heat, stirring occasionally.
3. Reduce heat to low and simmer for 30 minutes, or until the lingonberries are soft and the juice has thickened.
4. Strain the lingonberry juice into a clean glass jar and refrigerate for up to 2 weeks.

NUTRITIONAL FACTS

- Calories: 100
- Fat: 0g
- Carbohydrates: 25g
- Protein: 1g

Elderflower Cordial

Description: Elderflower cordial is a sweet and floral syrup that is made from elderflowers. It is a popular drink in Sweden and is often used to make cocktails and mocktails.

Ingredients

- 10 elderflower heads
- 1 liter (34 ounces) water
- 1 cup (200g) sugar
- 1 cup (250ml) lemon juice

Instructions

1. In a large saucepan, combine the elderflower heads, water, and sugar.
2. Bring to a boil over medium heat, stirring occasionally to dissolve the sugar.
3. Reduce heat to low and simmer for 30 minutes, or until the elderflower heads have wilted and the syrup has thickened.
4. Strain the elderflower cordial into a clean glass jar and stir in the lemon juice.
5. Refrigerate for up to 2 weeks.

NUTRITIONAL FACTS

- Calories: 100
- Fat: 0g
- Carbohydrates: 25g
- Protein: 0g

Raspberry Lemonade

Description: Raspberry lemonade is a refreshing and tart lemonade that is made with raspberries. It is a popular drink in Sweden and is often served during the summer months.

Ingredients

- 1 cup (200g) raspberries
- 1 cup (200g) sugar
- 1 cup (250ml) water
- 1 cup (250ml) lemon juice

Instructions

1. In a large saucepan, combine the raspberries, sugar, and water.
2. Bring to a boil over medium heat, stirring occasionally.
3. Reduce heat to low and simmer for 10 minutes, or until the raspberries have softened and the syrup has thickened.
4. Strain the raspberry syrup into a clean glass jar.
5. In a large pitcher, combine the raspberry syrup, lemon juice, and 4 cups (1 liter) of water.
6. Stir well and refrigerate for at least 2 hours before serving.

NUTRITIONAL FACTS

- Calories: 100
- Fat: 0g
- Carbohydrates: 25g
- Protein: 1g

Apple Cider

Description: Apple cider is a non-alcoholic beverage that is made from apples. It is a popular drink in Sweden and is often served during the fall and winter months.

Ingredients

- 1 gallon (4 liters) apple juice
- 1 cinnamon stick
- 10 cloves
- 1/2 teaspoon (2.5g) ground nutmeg

Instructions

1. In a large saucepan, combine the apple juice, cinnamon stick, cloves, and nutmeg.
2. Bring to a simmer over medium heat, stirring occasionally.
3. Reduce heat to low and simmer for 30 minutes, or until the apple cider is fragrant and flavorful.
4. Strain the apple cider into a clean glass jar and refrigerate for up to 2 weeks.

NUTRITIONAL FACTS
- Calories: 100
- Fat: 0g
- Carbohydrates: 25g
- Protein: 0g

Hot Chocolate

Description: Hot chocolate is a warm and comforting drink that is made with chocolate and milk. It is a popular drink in Sweden and is often served during the winter months.

Ingredients

- 1 cup (250ml) milk
- 1 tablespoon (15g) unsweetened cocoa powder
- 1 tablespoon (15g) sugar
- 1/4 teaspoon (1.25g) vanilla extract

Instructions

1. In a small saucepan, combine the milk, cocoa powder, sugar, and vanilla extract.
2. Bring to a simmer over medium heat, stirring occasionally.
3. Reduce heat to low and simmer for 5 minutes, or until the hot chocolate is smooth and creamy.
4. Serve hot.

NUTRITIONAL FACTS

- Calories: 150
- Fat: 5g
- Carbohydrates: 25g
- Protein: 5g

Eggnog

Description: Eggnog is a rich and creamy drink that is made with milk, eggs, sugar, and nutmeg. It is a popular drink in Sweden and is often served during the Christmas season.

Ingredients

- 1 dozen eggs
- 1 cup (200g) sugar
- 1 quart (1 liter) milk
- 1 cup (250ml) heavy cream
- 1 teaspoon (5g) ground nutmeg

Instructions

1. In a large bowl, whisk together the eggs and sugar until light and fluffy.
2. Gradually whisk in the milk and heavy cream.
3. Stir in the nutmeg.
4. Refrigerate for at least 2 hours before serving.

NUTRITIONAL FACTS

- Calories: 250
- Fat: 15g
- Carbohydrates: 30g
- Protein: 10g

CHAPTER 5: LIFESTYLE AND CULTURE

FIKA ETIQUETTE

Fika is a Swedish social custom that involves taking a break to enjoy coffee and pastries with friends or colleagues. It is an important part of Swedish culture and is often seen as a way to relax and socialize.

There are a few unwritten rules of fika etiquette that you should be aware of:

- **Always offer fika to guests.** It is considered rude to refuse an offer of fika.
- **Don't be in a hurry.** Fika is a time to relax and enjoy the company of others. Don't rush through your fika break.
- **Be social.** Fika is a social occasion, so make an effort to talk to the people you are with.
- **Don't talk about work.** Fika is a time to relax and socialize, so avoid talking about work.
- **Don't get drunk.** Fika is not a time to get drunk. It is a time to enjoy coffee and pastries with friends.

THE ART OF HYGGE

Hygge (pronounced "hoo-gah") is a Danish concept that refers to a feeling of coziness, contentment, and well-being. It is often associated with spending time with loved ones, enjoying simple pleasures, and creating a warm and inviting atmosphere.

There are many ways to create hygge in your life. Some popular hygge activities include:

Spending time with loved ones: Hygge is all about spending time with the people you care about. Whether you're having a dinner party, playing games, or just relaxing on the couch, spending time with loved ones is a surefire way to create a hygge atmosphere.

Enjoying simple pleasures: Hygge is also about enjoying the simple pleasures in life. This could mean anything from reading a good book to taking a walk in nature to baking a batch of cookies.

Creating a warm and inviting atmosphere: Your home should be a place where you feel comfortable and relaxed. Make sure your home is well-lit, decorated with things that you love, and filled with cozy textiles.

FIKA IN DAILY LIFE

Fika is an important part of daily life in Sweden. It is a time to relax, socialize, and enjoy the company of others. Fika can be enjoyed at any time of day, but it is most commonly enjoyed in the morning or afternoon.

There are many different ways to enjoy fika. Some popular fika activities include:

Having a coffee break with friends or colleagues: This is the most common way to enjoy fika. It is a great way to catch up with friends, chat with colleagues, or simply relax and enjoy a cup of coffee.

Going for a fika walk: This is a great way to enjoy the outdoors and get some exercise. Pack a thermos of coffee and some pastries and find a nice spot to sit and enjoy your fika.

Having a fika party: This is a great way to celebrate a special occasion or simply get together with friends and family. Serve coffee, pastries, and other fika treats, and enjoy the company of your guests.

FIKA AROUND THE WORLD

Fika is not just a Swedish phenomenon. It is a concept that is enjoyed all over the world. In fact, there are many different countries that have their own unique fika traditions.

Here are a few examples of fika around the world:

Denmark: In Denmark, fika is known as "hygge". Hygge is a similar concept to fika, but it is more focused on creating a cozy and inviting atmosphere.

Norway: In Norway, fika is known as "koselig". Koselig is a similar concept to fika and hygge, but it is more focused on spending time with loved ones.

Finland: In Finland, fika is known as "kahvi hetki". Kahvi Hetki is a similar concept to fika, but it is more focused on enjoying coffee and pastries.

Japan: In Japan, fika is known as "ochakai". Ochakai is a similar concept to fika, but it is more focused on the tea ceremony.

No matter where you are in the world, fika is a great way to relax, socialize, and enjoy the company of others. So next time you need a break, take a few minutes to enjoy a fika with friends or family.

CONCLUSION

Fika is more than just a coffee break. It is a social custom that is deeply ingrained in Swedish culture. It is a time to relax, socialize, and enjoy the company of others. Fika can be enjoyed in many different ways, from having a coffee break with friends to going for a fika walk to having a fika party.

No matter how you choose to enjoy it, fika is a great way to experience Swedish culture and connect with others. So next time you need a break, take a few minutes to enjoy a fika with friends or family.

Fika tips:

- Always offer fika to guests. It is considered rude to refuse an offer of fika.
- Don't be in a hurry. Fika is a time to relax and socialize. Don't rush through your fika break.
- Be social. Fika is a social occasion, so make an effort to talk to the people you are with.
- Don't talk about work. Fika is a time to relax and socialize, so avoid talking about work.
- Don't get drunk. Fika is not a time to get drunk. It is a time to enjoy coffee and pastries with friends.

The benefits of fika:

- Fika can help you to relax and de-stress.
- Fika can help you to socialize and connect with others.
- Fika can help you to learn about Swedish culture.
- Fika can help you to improve your Swedish language skills.
- Fika can help you to make new friends.

I hope you have enjoyed this book about fika. I encourage you to try fika for yourself and experience the many benefits it has to offer.

I'd love to hear what you think about my book. Your feedback is not just valuable, it's essential for my growth as an author. With your review, you're guiding not only me but also helping others decide if this book is right for them. Your words could be the beacon for someone's next favorite read. Thank you for being a part of my writing journey—I'm eagerly awaiting your thoughts.